The Me

TINDER

The Essential Manual For Tinder, Dating & Hookups

Chris Hemswith

Table of Contents

Introduction

Out with the old, in with the new

The Dating World.

Dating is alive and well here in the 21st century, even while this era gets criticized by the old guard for its lack of traditional romance. Now more than ever, people are meeting in the 'online' realm and while some people view this from a pedestal built upon every classic movie romance or novel they have ever consumed and cried over as some sort of dirty word, internet dating is becoming more and more of a success story for adult encounters and new couples coming together in these recent times.

Of course there is the undeniable charm in the notion of a chance meeting in some wildly romantic setting; Boy saves Girl from oncoming bus/ clutches of foreign crime gang (insert own dream scenario) however this desire tends to be reserved for those who actually believe that movie style romances come about on a daily basis and therefore wait patiently, mostly unsuccessfully, for one to land on their lap. But shouldn't we be identifying the sensible truth in all of these notions of romance and pairing up etc? The truth I am talking about is the notion that at the end of the day, the dream scene from your favorite rom-com is great but is the real victory not actually finding the right person rather than obsessing over the manner in which you meet?
I think this is overlooked by many men and women alike, and the falsehoods perpetrated by fictional romance has been slowly but fervently deconstructed in recent years by the upsurge in online dating success and the subsequent millions of people that use it. And not everyone is searching for the romantic stuff anyway!

Many people are embarrassed to divulge that they met their partner online, an outdated image or perception seems to still exist that meeting someone online has come as a result of desperation or lack of opportunities to meet someone conventionally. It's strange that this stigma is still so prevalent and causes people to be guarded about the beginning of their relationships that have begun from an online connection.

Anything short of a chance meeting of two people physically colliding in the street or the old fashioned guy approaches girl in a bar scenario involves some sort of facilitating agent, a catalyst. Blind dates need the mutual friend to set it up; people meeting in the work place have the work environment to thank. So, in fact, internet dating is merely providing that start point of two people interacting, it just happens that some people still see the use of such online devices as a little cold and unromantic. In terms of traditions and all our preconceptions about the romantic side of meeting new people, Tinder is rock bottom in the romance stakes in terms of its' layout and functions. However, in a purely percentage game of what gives you access to encountering new people and potential connections, there is nothing as powerful. Nothing.

Online dating has undeniable results. It might not be a miracle cure for all single people, but it does offer stepping stone into interacting with new people, which shouldn't be frowned upon. Now more that ever, people's lives in the western world are fast paced and highly competitive, careers and worries about money can make it difficult for single people to get enough regular social interactions that facilitate the formation of relationships or basic intimacy.

Why Choose Tinder? Because it works!

Typically, users that are new to Tinder have entered in with slight trepidation of using an online dating app, which Tinder has garnered some stigma due to its blasé approach to selecting and rejecting. The early incarnations of internet dating were fraught with people's general fear of the unknown. Chat rooms and dating forums were seen as the seedy backwaters of a suspicious world and even today with all the advances and breaking of boundaries, there is still a lingering stigma for people when they think of the prospect of meeting someone online as opposed to the old fashioned face to face way. However Tinder has none of the sinister elements that people associate with the darker side of internet dating. It is a simple and well structured app. Of course it's not going to be supermodel after supermodel that flash up on your screen, but no dating app gives you that assurance anyway. It is however arguably the most effective app environment combining speed and accessibility in connecting with the opposite sex.

My Own Experiences

On a personal level, Tinder has yielded a wide range of successes for me. I first encountered the app by becoming intrigued by my friend's account. I had been single for a while, and the combination of being hung up on an old ex of mine as well as not having a schedule that allowed me to be regularly meeting new people that much, convinced me to give it a shot. Once I harnessed the basic workings of the app and realized the best ways to put myself across with my profile, I found myself matching regularly with a range of different girls. Having a number of interactions on the app raised my confidence when talking to girls, honing my skills at initiating conversations, learning to develop good rapport and building the confidence to take the onward steps in asking girls out for dates.

Very soon the complications with my ex had all but evaporated and I was focused and excited about the interactions I was having.

Meeting with a number of girls through the app brought some really memorable nights, as well as a relationship for a while that was both unexpected and really fulfilling.
The success I had was not by chance, and the more I learned of the intricacies of the app and how I could make it work for my specific circumstances, the more I felt inclined to write this book and explore my findings. I had never been particularly proud of my skills when interacting with girls in the past, and now I found myself all of a sudden as a fairly accomplished operator, thanks to Tinder.

Expectations

Everyone has different tastes, different ideas and different desires for the type of encounters they are looking for; when it comes to Tinder users, they range from those with the simplest of desires, no-strings attached intimacy and no future aspirations with the individual, right up to people searching for a potential soul mate.
Within this book I will not be pointing judgmental fingers at anyone regarding romantic intentions or lack thereof; this is about making Tinder as an app work for you, and whether you're looking for a one night stand with a girl you never intend to see again or you're looking for the girl you'll spend the rest of your life with, the success ratio of your time on the app completely hinges on the same outcome; matches.

Throughout the course of the book, we will dissect the inner workings of Tinder and focus carefully on each and every aspect of your opportunities for personal input into your profile with a view to maximizing your success in matching with girls and the subsequent interactions with them that follow.

Regardless of who you are, where you're from, what you do for a living or what you look like, this guide to Tinder is aimed at creating the ideal personal profile that not only represents you best, but also compliments the workings of Tinder by identifying how your potential matches will be using the app and analyzing your

profile. By paying particularly close attention to habits of the girls who will be looking at your profile we will be able to tailor our profile specifically to maximize our attractiveness to the opposite sex, while presenting a true representation of ourselves.
While it is brutally uncompromising in its mechanisms for connections and rejections, for the savvy and prepared user it remains an indispensable resource for accessing new people.

Many of the girls on Tinder begin to use the app after recommendations from friends. While some have been successful in finding a relationship, many see it as a fun outlet to check out attractive guys as well as play about on the chat part. Regardless of their motivations for being on Tinder, we will explore the different girls you might encounter throughout your Tinder experience in this book. We will explore different trends and behavioral habits of female users with the hope of gaining a better understanding of how to assemble an interesting and engaging profile. From there we will explore the best ways to interact once we've connected with them in the hope of navigating through what can sometimes be a bit of a social minefield!

The key to success when it comes to online dating is the very acceptance that the process itself can in fact work for you and produce results. It's about embracing the mechanisms readily available and casting off preconceived prejudices and stigmas that have existed surrounding the subject. In the next chapter I will be delving into the workings of Tinder and the methods you can employ that will get you the best results as well as showing just how powerful the app can be for searching for potential dates and relationships.

Using Tinder To Win

The Quick History of Online Dating

Social life is not an endless commodity and though we often struggle to find as much time for it as we'd like, in recent years the online world has been adapting and innovating dating platforms to make finding potential relationships easier for people.
Before the significant advances in communication throughout the world, relationships were a product of an individual's immediate surroundings; people met their partners through family and friend networks, right from when humans first began creating settlements in which to develop agriculture. Fast forward x thousand of years to the advent of modern communications and transport, humans began interacting at an unprecedented level, with nothing more powerful than that of the creation of the internet. Connecting people became big business at the turn of the millennium; sites like the recently defunct Friends Reunited paved the way for connecting and re-connecting people on a mass scale. It has opened the way for countless social platforms since, with Facebook reinventing and dominating the landscape. However, internet dating was way ahead; the mid-nineties saw Match.com pioneer online dating for the first time and the idea of meeting a romantic match has been bubbling away in the psyche ever since. But it wasn't till some 17 years later that we saw the advent of the most powerful and unique dating tool ever seen by society. This was, of course, Tinder. It burst on to the dating scene with an incredibly straightforward user interface and a working mechanism, which provided people the opportunity to interact with romantic matches at a pace unseen before in the dating world.

The Essential Mechanisms

To begin using Tinder, you construct a basic profile like any other social media platform, generated through your Facebook account to provide pre existing data like your age, as well as details of your profession and education if you like. Your Facebook profile can also be used to outline basic aspects of you as a person with the use of pictures, short biographical elements and twinning your other social media profiles to allow girls to get a rough idea of who you are and what you look like.

Aside from recent innovations with premium accounts and various added functions, Tinder works on the simple premise of either liking someone or not, swiping someone's profile to the left if you're not keen, swiping right if you like them.
Swiping left sends the girl's profile off and out of your life just as looking away after a passing glance at someone on the street. However, swiping right can open the door to endless possibilities. By swiping right you log with Tinder that you like said girl, and if she just happens to like you as well, the magical **'IT'S A MATCH!'** appears on screen or you receive a notification once she swipes. This instantly connects the two of you via a chat window in which you can write to one another straight away with all the functionality of your existing social platforms, except you're there for one reason only, that you have both liked each other.
It's really that simple. From there a whole batch of new challenges await but we'll get on to those later in the book. In the next chapter we'll be focusing on assembling the ideal elements for your profile to give you the best chance at getting matches.

The design of the app is so specifically geared towards speedy activity and superficial based decisions that there isn't much encouragement from the app to delve that deep into someone's personality initially. This is not to say that Tinder is an inherently evil application, simply that the workings of the app are tuned specifically towards quick analysis of faces and some basic written descriptions you can choose to add as well. You'll find the pace of your swiping will probably increase and in no time you'll be scrolling past reams of girls faces, pausing only for ones that catch your eye. So you must bear in mind that this is how girls will mostly be operating as well. This is a huge consideration because if you are aware that girls are stopping only for guys they deem interesting or good looking enough, then how you present yourself on the surface of your personal profile will be absolutely critical in the frequency of their right swipes in your favor.

The Super Like

There is a third preference option that was introduced recently called the 'Super Like' where a user can opt to swipe upwards; this attaches a notification to that user when they encounter the person who Super Liked them. It breaks the traditional Tinder mechanism and introduces a third dimension to outcomes. Before, when you swiped right on someone you either matched with them or you never found out whether they didn't like you or just didn't ever see your profile.

With the Super Like, you can now profess your interest directly to a girl, as she swipes through her list of men, your profile will appear in blue showing that you have super liked them. She now has the knowledge of this and will choose whether to swipe you away, to simply like you or Super Like you back. While it allows you to tell someone you find them especially attractive, it leaves you open to the clear knowledge of rejection if she doesn't return your affection. The super like is limited to just one per day however, unless you opt to pay a premium plan in order to get more Super Likes and other features that manipulate the traditional workings of the app in your possible favor.

Play The Game To Win!

So before you hastily sign up and get swiping, the thing to be aware of is that there is an entire world of strategy and planning to actually succeed with Tinder. Yes, you can be on there within five minutes of setting the app up, but if you truly want to harness the power of Tinder, it's better to analyze its workings as well as consider how girls are using the app before you put yourself out there.

How Tinder *Really* Works

The key functionality of Tinder is speed. Quick to show you girls, instantly matching you with a girl if you have both swiped right, then instantly opening a platform for you to converse.

So if you imagine a girl swiping through endless swathes of hopeful suitors like yourself, then you can see that she can afford to be picky. Really picky. This isn't debutante ball era stuff; this is modern day lightning fast dating on an industrial scale. Just as you will scan the very basic elements of each girls profile, she will be doing the same.

The big difference is that most guys are dazzled and drawn in by bright lights, big boobs and makeup, and this superficial aspect to guys' choices is a very different landscape to the complex preferences that the girls reserve for choosing us.

Men and women perceive each others profiles differently on the app, and it is vital to be aware of these distinctions when considering your own approach to setting up the elements of your profile. For example where a pretty girl with a profile picture in her low cut top amasses truck loads of right swipes, you with a topless gym selfie or something of the equivalent will more than likely garner you distain from the majority of the female Tinder world. Girls want sophistication, sincerity and confidence in a guy; you in a vest and a squat rack in the back of the picture won't achieve this!

We have all heard the long pedaled notion that guys are turned on by what they see and girls by what they hear. While that rule is slightly skewed on Tinder, most of that statement remains true. As she claps eyes on your profile for that split second, the only elements preventing her from swiping you left into oblivion are extremely finite. Profile picture and a short bio. She is assessing and deciding on you in a split second so it is absolutely imperative that what she sees in that time makes her hover over the screen, hesitating as something or a combination of aspects of your profile hold her attention. Girls, on average, swipe right much less than men so as a guy you're faced with the pickier of the two sexes.

In the next chapter we will be getting into the real detailing of how to construct a winning profile to catch the eye of would-be matches.

Why Tinder?

Tinder might have courted some controversy by what some have perceived as an outwardly simplified and shallow selection process based primarily on looks, but that is really just on the surface. Unlike a lot of other dating sites, Tinder doesn't ask for a multitude of stats to input into some sort of algorithm to determine your compatibility with an individual, it allows you to determine that for yourself. And perhaps knowledge of the mathematical compatibility might not always benefit you in your pursuit of happiness. With a site like OK Cupid, one of its profile requirements when setting up is a fairly extensive line of questioning in order to match you up with the most suited person and while it helps weed out people who have vastly different views to yourself, it undoubtedly elevates the expectation of a match going well when you embark on your conversation.

The beauty of Tinder is that in terms of parameters, the only ones that exist are the ones you choose to limit your potential matches with. The only comparisons that Tinder will generate are the number of Facebook likes you have in common, and that in itself is positive data. Any other comparisons or conclusions that are drawn will be made entirely by each user when assessing someones profile. You alone are making the decisions on someone and not being influenced by an algorithm. This lack of restriction allows you to draw your own conclusions about compatibility; you may stick strictly to the morals and preferences you have developed throughout your life and choose potential matches like that or you might see the attraction in someone who has different views or interests and be intrigued by their way of life. You might encounter someone of a different race or creed that you may never had any contact with before. Whatever your angle or approach to Tinder, it facilitates access to a plethora of girls without recommending who it thinks you should or shouldn't be compatible with.

Does Tinder Actually Work?

Conduct

Whether you're looking to hook up with an anonymous girl for the night or whether you're on the look out for that one special girl, it's important to maintain a level of decency throughout your conduct on Tinder. Conducting yourself in a respectful way should be a given in all aspects of life, but it is often forgotten and the male mentalities are difficult things to tame in many situations, whether it's getting involved in a fight or making a remark about a girls appearance in the street that makes her feel uncomfortable. Unfortunately when behind a screen like we have seen exhibited by the keyboard warrior and troll generation of internet users these days, people can act appallingly from the safety of their computers or devices. This behavior is often magnified in the online dating realm as there is the added expectation from users on it hoping to find nice people to interact with, as well as often putting themselves in a vulnerable position to be insulted or belittled by insensitive users who have no interest in taking the persons feelings sensitively.

Even an app with such low relative success rate (right swipes compared with left swipes) Tinder has certain functionality that prevents the feeling of rejection. For instance, you never really know why someone that you swiped right on never matched with you. You never find out conclusively whether they swiped you left or just never saw your profile. So in that way your ego is protected by the unknown, which is probably a good thing! No one is ever going to benefit from that sort of knowledge of rejection.

The less gentle side of Tinder lies in the functionality of it's chat interface. Once you have matched with someone you both have the power to terminate the conversation and block that person at any time with no fear of reprisal. This is a useful aspect as it prevents the invasive nature of some abusive users, however in the case of a conversation going well with one person having more emotions at stake than the other, it does put the dominant user in an unusually powerful position of being able to go silent, and abandon that person on the other side. It happens a lot and it is something that we must be prepared to endure as well as be mindful of if we ever entertain the ides of doing it ourselves. Tinder may to some be a fun and trivial pastime, where to others it is their genuine attempt to search for a suitable person to have a relationship with. So no matter what your motivation and expectation for what the app can bring, be mindful that the person on the other end might not see it from your point of view. (In other words, don't be a dick!)

Profile Setup – The Vital Rules To Get It Right

If you walk up to a girl in a bar and offer to buy her a drink, and end up striking up conversation without coming across like a serial killer, the chances are she will have a good first impression of you; you have exhibited an interest in her and shown that in a confident way. There are also many little gestures or mannerisms that you might display that she happens to like, or even simply the sound of your voice. With Tinder, her first impression of you will be solely based upon your pictures and a short bio. So the images and words that you choose to put down are pivotal in her assessment of you as a person and possible match.

Maximizing your success from Tinder comes down to controlling the first impression that you project from your profile and the subsequent chat that you have with your matches.

Play It Smart

We all have our insecurities; some of us might feel we're not particularly attractive, that we don't have a very powerful job or that we don't have interesting pastimes.

You might not exactly feel anything like a real life James Bond, but by carefully assembling the right elements for a profile, anyone can produce an attractive and genuine profile that shows the aspects of your lifestyle that will hold the girls attention for that split second longer. Remember, a lot of the time, the biggest hurdle of guys on Tinder is simply getting the girl to stop long enough on their profile to consider NOT swiping left.

There is no magical equation or combination for the most effective bio, however there are some direct paths to instant rejection that are easily avoided.

A girl is going to assess you in a number of main stages on Tinder and most likely in this order:

1. Her initial reaction to your main profile picture
2. A glance at your bio, (age, profession, short description of yourself)
3. Looking further into your other pictures
4. Likes in common
5. Your external links (instagram etc)

So as you can see there are such limited opportunities to sell yourself with your profile on Tinder, that's why it's very important to carefully consider each and every aspect of what your potential matches are going to end up seeing of you.

Of course, if you wanted to, you could save yourself a bit of time, slap up a picture and leave everything blank. However the maverick technique puts many girls off due to lack of information and is reserved for only the best looking and photogenic guys.

In reality, most of us won't fall into that coveted category, and we need to give some consideration to those other elements mentioned above. In the next chapter we will look into the art and psychology behind pictures, what types look best and what sort of content can help you maximize your matching potential.

The Pictures – The Part Most Guys Mess Up!

Whether we like it or not, your main photo on Tinder is going to be the single most important aspect of your profile and it should be given a lot of consideration before you even think of starting to swipe. So many first impressions in life are based on the visual aspect and Tinder is especially so. The user is making initial split second judgments based almost entirely on what they see in the lead picture. The tendency on Tinder is to swipe left at a high rate and only stop for a split second when a face or a particular element of the picture catches their eye long enough to halt the rapid rejection of profiles. With this in mind, we will explore the various elements that make up a winning lead photo, then moving onto the five other spaces available for additional photos and what constitutes good content.

People who are deemed more 'conventionally attractive' undoubtedly receive more interest and have more right swipes with more subsequent matches. Their *initial* success will be little to do with anything other than their pictures. The favorable treatment of people with good looks is just how the landscape of our world is and has been for generations. However a key consideration is that Tinder isn't just a platform for people with outstanding good looks and you aren't excluded for not meeting some sort of visual criteria. What it does do is provide an environment for anyone (18 years old and above) a chance at matching and conversing with everyone within their chosen parameters, regardless of looks.

Get This Element Right and You Are On The Road To Success!

The main picture! As this is the first image a potential match is going to see of you, it has to be your most considered and well constructed image. Regardless of any other content that your main picture might incorporate, you should show yourself in a clear and well lit image. Your potential match will be assessing you on a split second judgment, two questions they will quickly answer for themselves are:

- 'Has his picture caught my eye?'
- 'Do I find him attractive?'

For these reasons be sure you have selected the most interesting picture combined with the clearest indication of your looks. The picture should be flattering but ***realistic***. This is not the stage to be heavily photoshopping your features in the hope she's going to instantly fall in love with you, the first thing she sees shouldn't be, and nor should any other elements of your profile EVER be, misleading.

The shirtless selfie with a weights bench in the background will only show you as a one-dimensional narcissist, no matter how genuine your love for fitness is. A girl is looking for a guy who will be interested in her and not obsessed with his own appearance! That's not to say you shouldn't use a picture that shows off your physical appearance, it is the manner in which you present it which has a crucial effect on how girls will view you. So by all means if you're confident with your body and appearance, don't be afraid to incorporate it, the key is to be subtle about it. A candid, non posed picture of you is infinitely better in those cases.

On the flip side of that, if you don't have what you perceive to be the perfect body, don't feel pressured with the thought that it's the key to catching a girls eye, because it's not.

Have fun with your lead picture! 99% of the time, surprisingly, a girl will be more attracted to a guy who can make her laugh than anything else. The picture should be eye-catching and stand out from the crowd, some guys use photos of them in an everyday environment, some guys put their face onto Godzilla's body breathing fire onto the side of a terrified building full of people. Your main profile picture should best reflect your personality. So if you're a bit of a goofball in general, you might feel like the jokey angle best illustrates your personality. If you are a focused person who rates their career high in their identity then portray yourself in that environment. Or if your main passion is the outdoors and you can't wait to get away from the office and escape to the wilderness at weekends then show a picture of yourself there. Be yourself. Own it. Don't lie. Don't be fake. It will not work. Really. This advice goes for any particular passion, don't be afraid to show the side of you that makes you happiest just be sure to display it in an eye-catching way.

The Other Pictures – The Followup!

Although the main picture that appears first when girls see your profile is by far the most important aspect of your profile, the others are vital in strengthening the overall image of you.
Sincerity is a hugely valuable asset when it comes to Tinder. The sooner your potential match can get a sense of your personality, the more likely she is to give you a chance. Bland and nondescript images will be passed over in most cases unless you're Hugh Jackman in a speedo. (***actually*** Hugh Jackman, not someone who looks like him…). With the 6 picture allocations there is no point using 6 identical head shots; any girl that takes the time to look over your profile is going to be intrigued enough that they will want to get a bit of a sense of who you are. Therefore your pictures should at least paint a bit of a picture as to who you are by showing diversity to your character, your profession, your interests and any other sort of indicators.

The following examples of types of photos that are used are a good start when deciding on how you want to portray yourself on Tinder; not every example will apply to your particular situation and don't feel pressured to use up all 6 spaces on your photo section. Anywhere from 3 or more pictures will help to present a bit of an insight into your life and character.

Active
If you are sporty or simply enjoy the outdoors, a picture showing this is a big plus. Showing broad interests or particular activities helps increase the chances of some common ground between you and the girl. Initial connections between people always advance quicker when there are common interests to strike up conversation about. If you're just looking for a hook up, it's good to at least be able to have something to talk about, and if you're searching for a relationship, finding a match with similar interests makes the likelihood of a relationship blossoming increase massively. For example, if you are big into trail running and you come across a girl who seems equally passionate, aren't you glad that you had a photo of you running in the first place? The chances are that she saw your profile and liked

the look of you initially, but her motivation to swipe right probably came when she saw you had a common interest.

Specific Interests

The genuine portrayal of your lifestyle and interests will always be your strongest suit when showing yourself on Tinder, aside from perhaps revealing information about a life of crime or membership of some militia group, but then hey, some girls like a dangerous guy!

The Tux

Girls are suckers for a guy in a suit. So if you happen to have any particularly dashing photos from a wedding or other formal occasion, or simply a good work suit, it's going to pay dividends. Remember, each photo has the potential to speak volumes to the person looking at them. A potential match who sees you in a Tux or a suit will automatically associate you having sophistication and a decent social standing. Photos like these should be natural and not deliberately composed otherwise you run the risk of coming across as some guy that hired a suit just for the photo!

Travel

Travel excites most people. It opens our eyes to different ways of life, cultures and experiences. Pictures of you in far flung places will add another dimension to your profile. Travelling shows life experience of places and other cultures and generally shows initiative and drive in a person. You might not be a jet-setting pilot travelling the world every day but any recent or past travel experiences will be just as an intriguing prospect for a potential match. Showing pictures of travel also help to add authenticity to your story. A profile with one picture and no description can often be viewed with suspicion. *'Why does he not have any information up, why only one picture, what is he hiding?'.*

These anxieties that potential matches might have from lack of information can be easily avoided through even the slightest bit of variety.

Animals

While this tactic is a little crude, there is no mistaking the power of cute animals. A picture of you holding something like a cute puppy is an inescapable draw for girls, it shows a gentle and caring side to your personality. Mixing up various elements will work well; you can combine elements such as an animal picture with a travel photo. You holding a lion cub on safari somewhere in Africa would be a pretty strong look. Don't start looking for baby lions though…

Babies?

Only if they are yours. The resounding answer on this topic is that any photos of you with a baby or child will instantly give the impression you have your own kids. Tinder is a world based on snap judgments and unless you are in fact a parent and looking for someone in the same position or someone who is actively open to dating a single parent, it is better to avoid pictures with babies. Unfortunately it can be a real turn off for a lot of people if you are in fact childless and could seriously impact upon your successes on the app without you even knowing it. It's certainly not a pretty fact, but a fact nonetheless.

Friends

A picture or two with groups of friends shows your social side and ability to mix well with people. A whole collection of group pictures however will make it frustratingly difficult, if not impossible, to pick you out from the crowd so avoid overkill on it. I would especially recommend not using group photos as your lead picture as a girl is far more likely to make a positive initial judgment on your profile picture if it's just you. The last thing you want is her to find one of your friends attractive then suffer the disappointment that you're in fact the other guy. It is a common mistake to make!

Opposite Sex

Pictures beside another girl or group of girls is a bit of a minefield. Yes she might be your sister but in a split second assessment of your profile, a potential match might not wish to delve any further. Remember girls are territorial creatures and aren't looking to compete for you with another girl (aka: a perceived threat).

Family

Similarly to the group photos with friends, family photos show a genuine side to your life and helps put girls at ease that you're not some serial killer drifter who happens to have a smart phone. Photos with your parents and siblings are great but as I stated above, a photo of just you and your sister might be misconstrued.

Reality

Remember it's not about being a millionaire celebrity with a chiseled body on Tinder! Those things obviously will attract girls, but as much as some females might desire fantastical images of a guy that they are bombarded with in film and media, common ground and relatable experiences will draw a girls eye just as much.

Are my pictures any good?

By now you should have a good idea about what are good pictures to use for your profile, as well as elements that you should be avoiding. A good way to put your choices to the test is to get a girls opinion on your photos and profile in general. A womans perspective is very useful in identifying any misguided or ill-thought out choices of content. Don't do anything silly like asking your Mom, she loves every picture of you, it is her job! Instead, an honest and close female friend would be the perfect litmus test for your potential profile. Treat it almost like a test run and you will be able to gain a unique angle on how your profile might be perceived once going live. Tell her she can be totally honest about her reactions to your pictures. Only absolute honesty will stop you from making any poor choices.

However, before you jump straight in and start swiping with just photos up, we're going to look at the other side to the tinder profile, the Bio. This area, while playing second string to your profile pictures, will be a crucial component in convincing the girl that has hovered over your picture for a second to give you a chance. Where the pictures have shown her what you look like and other visual sides to your life, the written element of your profile will help give a more rounded view of your lifestyle and help reinforce what she is seeing in your pictures.

Writing The Perfect Bio

By a glance at the bio, I mean that in a literal sense. If she has indeed stopped once seeing your picture and is willing to make a further judgment on you with the bio, it will be only a momentary pause, such is the rate and volume at which users scroll through potential matches.

The bio section can be an area that causes uncertainty in users of how best to put themselves across. Using this small window on your profile effectively can be a daunting task. It is the one place girls will read about you, and with a 500 character limit you have to be brief in establishing a good description of yourself. The fast paced nature of Tinder gears the user towards making quick decisions, therefore your bio should contain quick and easy to understand information.

Not everyone has an exciting and prestigious job with a six-figure income to show off to the world but that shouldn't prevent you from talking about yourself. As much as girls are dazzled by the glamour and success of someone, a rich guy who comes across as a cocky asshole is only going to attract similarly shallow women and put off the rest. Tinder is an app based solely on first impressions to determine matches however the majority of girls, whether just looking for a hook up or looking for a relationship, are searching for genuine guys behind these profiles. As much as a girl will assess a guy on his looks, physical prowess and career, a guy that can make them laugh and come across as genuine and be likely to treat women with respect and courtesy are going to be successful, despite their shortcomings in other departments. And this goes for girls looking for both relationships and just casual hookups!

Beyond The Visual

As I touched on earlier in the chapter when discussing the key mechanisms of Tinder, the other elements you can use to put yourself across are extremely finite and as result, are much more likely to be taken on board and considered by a potential match.

You might consider yourself as a pretty average looking guy, or even that you're way below the bar, and while Tinder might be off putting as it is so visually geared, there are great advantages to be had through the other parts of your profile:

Profession

A lot of guys leave this out as they are worried how they will be perceived. However in most cases disclosing your job title will help give your potential match more of a sense of the type of the person you are. A high status profession in law or finance will not just allude to your earning power but also your strength of character and intelligence, not to mention the amount of hard work and dedication that it would have taken to reach the career that you are in. On the other hand you might work a more regular minimum wage job and while that might put off girls in search of a guy in a more prestigious career, you're still disclosing information that helps the girl get a sense of who you are. Remember you might just attract someone in a similar field as a result. Don't forget, Tinder may work mostly off the visual aspect but beyond her initial assessment of you, information about yourself might just sway her to swiping right. Common ground is a great asset in this game!

Education

Education allows your match to judge you on your capabilities as well as opening yourself up to the possibility of having common ground. You may view your education days as a foggy distant memory or an arduous stressful time but to a potential match it allows her to find common ground. Perhaps her friends went to the same university as you did or perhaps went there herself. Common ground between strangers will always make them more at ease whether you find the information out face to face or behind a screen.

How To Write A Winning Bio

The key considerations for bio content are as follows:

Don't leave it blank!

This is a huge error made by countless guys. Some don't see any relevance in writing something for various reasons which include them being worried about writing the wrong thing, or in an attempt to come across as a little mysterious and letting their pictures do the talking. This is a highly risky tactic; girls are far more inclined to consider you if they read even the slightest bit of interesting information about you. And if they were in any doubt at all about whether they were attracted to you or not, the absence of a Bio will all but certainly condemn you to getting swiped left, almost every time.

Get to the point, fast!

Be direct with descriptions of yourself. You want the girl to feel like she wants to start a conversation with you. You might have a boring or unremarkable sounding job, but perhaps at weekends you love to go rock climbing with friends, so emphasize the latter. If you are truly passionate about something in your life, talk about it, there is no better way to show an authentic aspect of your personality than to put it center-stage on your bio.

Strong Views

Be wary when citing any overtly politically or religious views unless you are intentionally ruling out any opposing views or hoping to only attract those that share yours; strong ideologies tend to put off most even keeled people right from the beginning. The beauty of Tinder is in its ability to connect you with a huge variety of girls from all walks of life and backgrounds but the downside is that a divisive or heavily opinionated bio can rule you out of a massive cross section of the Tinder world.

Lay off the Negatives

Some guys use the bio section as a platform to vent their frustrations at particular negative traits that some girls show on their profiles, things like 'swipe left if you're a posey self-absorbed vacuous duck face etc etc'. The premise behind this tactic is to show a strong ethical ideology, or at the very least, being incredibly opinionated. The *reality* unfortunately is that it just gives off a general negative vibe and while you might score points for honesty, you're going to put off more girls than you will attract. The mechanism of Tinder is designed to give you full control over who you accept or decline, and those negative attributes you are attempting to weed out can be eliminated from your own assessment of each girl, not by building your own barrier/ vetting system on your own profile.

Education and Profession

These aspects to your background can be incredibly powerful attributes to your profile. Status and social standing in men is a huge turn on for women and the attraction runs deeper than just being dazzled by a suit, they are sizing you up as a potential mate and well paid, high powered jobs and good education all contribute to her assessment of you being dependable and protective of her. Within the online dating world, there are niche market apps aimed directly at people in these demographics who wish to interact specifically with people of their own intellectual and financial standing. Tinder does not draw such distinctions or exclusions and simply allows users the option to disclose such information if they wish to let potential matches of that side of their background. So it would be foolish not to disclose these attributes on your profile, as they are extremely desirable in most cases. That being said, not everyone has a high powered job or went to a prestigious school in which case a little bit of honesty is good but perhaps the old adage of "less is more" is worth baring in mind here.

Humble is the Key

If you view yourself as interesting and fun to be around, don't actually write it in the bio! Stating opinion-based attributes in words will only make her question them and make you sound like you're saying 'I'm a really great catch I have so much going for me'. These positive sides to your personality are much more effectively and sincerely depicted through the images you put up and through the subsequent conversation you strike up with your match. The key is to not get ahead of yourself in an attempt to fast track her opinion of you.

The top two attributes most commonly cited by women as being the most positive elements of a guy's bio have been sincerity and humor. This speaks volumes in terms of what general parameters you work within when considering your biographical content.

Humor

Humor is an incredibly powerful attribute in guys when it comes to attracting girls. We all know of that one friend who although isn't the best looking guy in the world will still end up chatting to the most women on a night out. Humor and playfulness is a huge advantage in the dating world, women see it as a non-aggressive trait in men. It's a primal instinct in women in order to secure a successful mate and a protector of offspring. We aren't living in caves anymore but the rules are the same. In the dating world this translates to if you are funny and interesting, you stand a much greater chance of success.

Be Sincere

Of course you could create a profile consisting of a combination of the mostly desirable characteristics that you could imagine a girl would like. You could easily put up a photo of a male model, say you were extremely wealthy, devote a lot of time to charitable works and child welfare and then go skydiving or wrestle crocodiles at the weekend to let off steam. You would probably garner a huge amount of matches and be enticing countless attractive women. But then of course at some point in the conversation your cover would be blown as she delves deeper into her questions about your lifestyle and you would be exposed as a fraud, receiving a swift block on your chat. Or worse still, you might evade her suspicions right till your first face to face meeting and have to suffer the indignity of back-pedaling and become the butt of her subsequent date story amongst her appalled friends.

So rather than becoming a dating horror story statistic, the obvious choice is to be genuine. Always. Don't listen to the bullshit pick-up artists. That nonsense never works. NEVER. And don't forget, there is a legion of idiots out there who are rude, crass and overtly sexual to their matches. Simply by you being cordial and friendly without any of the bullshit macho overtones, you'll very much stand out from that crowd and stand a much better chance of success.

Likes In Common

While the photo and written bio sections of your profile are useful in potential matches getting an insight into your appearance and personality, another very effective way of establishing common ground is through your likes in common. This appears on your Tinder profile direct from your personal liked pages on your Facebook. So if you have any common likes they will show up when you go to view each others profiles. If you don't happen to like any particular pages on your Facebook already, I'd highly recommend spending a bit of time dong it. Favorite music, films, TV shows, sports and any other relevant activities to your life, ones that you feel represent you as a person. Don't just like things for the sake of it or begin liking things in the hope you think they will appeal to your potential matches. Not only is this misleading it will also get you caught out if any subsequent conversation lands on the subject.

Instagram

The addition of being able to link your Instagram account was a response to an upsurge in users leaving links to their social media accounts on their bios as a way for potential matches to see more content. The more cynical view was that some users were using Tinder as a platform in order to garner higher numbers of followers on their Twitter, Snapchat and Instagram accounts. However, Tinder bowed to this pressure trend and twinned with Instagram in its Bio section.

From the outside it may look like having your Instagram account (if you have one) available to view on your profile provides more detail for potential matches to vet you. It can be argued that it is a positive thing as it allows a potential match to get a sense of who you are and what your lifestyle is…but there is also cause to believe that it actually *doesn't*. The problem with too much content on your profile, especially with something like your Instagram accountis that it will reveal all your posts to your potential matches and this increases the chances that they may stumble across something that they don't like; an extremely drunken picture you put up two years ago for laugh, photos of ex-girlfriends or just other girls (big no no!) or simply an aspect of your life that hasn't been clearly enough explained and puts them off. Be careful with what you post! (which in a lot of ways should be true for any social media account).

The Bio: The Factor That Will Make or Break You!

The reason why Tinder has been so successful has in part been down to how it is constantly evolving and trying new aspects to add to the experience, but the real win has come from the core user interface that runs on a limited profile with few elements. This has meant keeping the selection picking fast and a certain level of mystique to each user that can often benefit and sway someone into liking you.

Basically what I'm saying is that less is more in this case! Six of your very best photo selections, details about your job and a well thought out written bio section allow you to form a direct and succinct calling card that maximizes your visibility and desirability within the confines of an app that runs mainly on initial assessments and quick decisions. Those are the core strengths you can work to and getting the basics right are the key to a successful profile.

The Girls Of Tinder

How To Deal With Different Girls & Get What You Want

Women are complex beings. In many ways they remain a mystery to us men through their vastly different ways of perceiving the world from ourselves. We chase them around the schoolyard when we are at junior school then become completely fixated on them as soon as we hit puberty. From there to young adult life and beyond it takes a masterful mind and many years of trial and error to figure out even the smallest intricacies and identifying the differences between us when it comes to understanding the fairer sex. We approach all manner of problem solving differently. We are lone wolves at heart and sometimes like to work through issues ourselves while women seek advice and share problems in order to tackle them more thoroughly.

We communicate differently. While we converse in simpler terms, women are much more tuned in to body language, facial expressions and tone. This is not opinion, it is scientifically proven. And while women perceive interactions and problems with emotional attachment, men tend to operate on a much more practical level with emotional implications being much less critical to lifes analysis. Even with the knowledge of these key differences in the sexes and the ability to anticipate the actions of our potential match, we will still be governed by our own hardwired responses to dealing with interactions.

With Tinder, girls will have many different backgrounds as well as motivations for using the app. These motivations lead to a subsequent trend in their behavior and how they act on it. The following examples are by no means hard and fast stereotypes of girls but they offer some insight into what to expect when you encounter matches.

Disclaimer! This is a broad and generalizing sub-section. Of course girls aren't always going to fit exactly into these stringent categories but it's a useful way to display the sorts of behavior you will encounter on Tinder.

<u>The Hook up</u>

- Direct and looking for physical contact
- Recent freedom from a bad relationship
- Craving contact with guys
- Open to harnessing whatever opportunities the app can bring
- Selections made primarily on looks/ status/ base attractions

While most men could probably have their arm twisted to do a one night stand, girls are much less likely to be convinced to have one, let alone be actively looking for such a fleeting and emotionless hook up. So *Hook up girl* will be quite a rarity. And she might not be that easy to spot. The assumption would be that a girl looking for a hookup would be all high heels, low cut tops and flaunting their figures. However those girls are just as likely to be looking to be wined and dined as opposed to simply looking for intimacy. Hook up girls can be unassuming and subtler in their appearance. They could be busy career women who don't have time or any desire to spend a lot of time conversing or dating. We all have desires and although the two sexes are vastly different in our approach to interacting with each other, sometimes sex itself is the sole motivation for a person matching.

A guys motivation for a one night stand is much more likely to be because they're horny while a girls desire for unattached intimacy can come from more complex places. She could be just out of a stifling long-term relationship and is so keen to explore experiences with other men that she feels she has been missing out on. Or she could have been at the end of a bad run of dating guys for potential relationships and she is tired of investing time into serious pursuits and just wants a bit of fun. A girl with the no strings attached approach is far more likely to be open to Tinder and how it works, not concerning herself with disapproving spectators but more open to whatever opportunities might present themselves from matching. Pursuing just a hook up, she is more likely to make choices on the app based solely on appearance and less concerned with a guys background or hobbies. She will enjoy interactions with multiple matches but when it comes to meeting in person she will still be just as selective as any girl. She will lose interest with a conversation that meanders and goes nowhere so you will need to be engaging and confident, moving relatively quickly to make plans to meet in person.

Just Browsing

- Encouraged by friends experiences on it
- No expectation of the app, just fun
- Enjoys interaction with guys and seeing the variety
- No real intention on meet ups except in particularly intriguing circumstances
- Selections a combination of looks and entertaining/ exciting bios

Just Browsing is self-explanatory. She is a confident girl who has no trouble meeting guys in the outside world and has got the app purely for the fun element. Just like the other types of girls, she enjoys the interaction with guys she matches with but has little or no interest or even aspirations to pursue anything further. Tinder is not a dating tool for her and she will use it for amusement and validation for as long as she sees fit. The browsing girl will not have spent a great deal of time or consideration on her profile, a few pictures and short description will be all she is operating with. Girls who list more details or parameters to their bios are purposely being more specific in order to weed out any time wasters.

After a match, even if Browser Girl does continue dialogue with a particular match or even takes the plunge to meet up in person, she has no expectations of it going anywhere. Don't be completely put off by this girl however; she is looking to interact with interesting guys. A profile with exciting photos and an engaging bio will entice her and hey, you might even be the one to dispel her lack of belief in the power of the app!

You might be there for the same reason, to simply interact with the opposite sex without any massive expectation of what might transpire with a match. I would always say approach with an open mind. You might think there is no way the app could yield a meaningful interaction or possibly lead to sex, but at the end of the day it is all down to the chemistry between two people. Tinder simply provides an arena to meet; there are infinite possibilities with what can happen subsequently. I met a girl just browsing and we ended up dating for two years in a fantastic relationship.

The See-What-Happens Girl

- Selections are a combination of looks and entertaining/ exciting bios
- Has no real agenda for what she is looking for but is very open to ideas

As with most new Tinder users, there is still a little residual suspicion about the nature of the app and its perception in the dating world. The *see-what-happens girl* has taken the plunge and gone into it with an open mind. She may well have been single for a while for various reasons such as a busy career with little time for socializing or maybe she had some uninspiring dating experiences till now and has taken on Tinder to see if it what everyone else says it is. She won't have massive expectations about any potential success it could bring but she is willing to put herself out there and interact and possibly meet with new guys. She is probably the most rounded of our Tinder girls in her approach to analyzing potential matches. She is likely to assess them with a mixture of looks and personal interests so a well-rounded profile is especially important in this instance. For this type of girl your profile as a whole will be particularly important. She herself will have put a lot of thought into her own profile, presenting a rounded image of herself, particularly emphasizing her interests as a way of attracting like minded guys. If she is going to potentially meet up with a guy she would rather it be leading somewhere and will be avoiding dead ends with guys she has nothing in common with.

The Wedding Dress

- Using the app expressly to look for a relationship

- Especially keen to find guys that share things/ views in common/ common goals
- Selects less on looks, more analytical of bio details and common ground

The *wedding dress girl*, who avoids the uncertainties of the single life. She thrives within the security of relationships and will often pursue potential matches without too much consideration into how mismatched the pairing might be. If you are matching with this type of girl then the bets are she has left her last relationship recently and is now resolute in filling the void that single life brings with it. You, or any of her matches, could be the next guy, given that you appear to have the appropriate credentials and while it might not be immediately evident from her pictures, they certainly will by her bio. It will reflect this specific desire to find a relationship and you're certainly not going to confuse her with the Hook Up girl! The written elements to her bio will carry a strong message about her intentions on the app. She has perhaps been using Tinder for a while and encountered mismatches by not making her intentions clear enough and will have updated the tone of her bio to make sure guys are well informed.

The main angle the wedding dress girl is working from is simply to find a relationship with someone who is well matched and not wasting time. She will be particularly interested in the bio aspects of guys. She will really inspect the profiles, carefully assessing compatibility of age, career and lifestyle with her own. If you yourself are in the market for the same sort of thing then don't leave yourself at a disadvantage by having scant details on your own profile. The greater the picture you can paint of your own lifestyle the more chance you'll have at similarly minded girls taking an interest in you.

At the end of the day, identifying the desires of your potential match early on is a huge bonus and will help you align yourself with like-minded girls and save you a lot of time on mismatched endeavors. Simply put, if you're just looking for sex, you don't want to mindlessly be putting the moves on every match you encounter, and on the other side of the coin, if you're looking for a meaningful relationship to develop, don’t go chasing the party girl who is looking for some gratification for the night!

How To Overcome The Obstacles

While doing research for this book an essential part of gathering expertise and knowledge was to talk to guys who had had a lot of success with the app as well as guys who had none at all. When attempting to quantify success on the app, a good place to start was to ask users who had little or no luck to see if there were any patterns or causes.

One such guy I interviewed, Martin, had used the app for a few months with no success and got rid of it, but had agreed to restart his profile for mutually beneficial purposes, in that I could test my findings as well he could have another shot at the Tinder world. An average looking guy who was quite sociable and had a good job should have had at least some success on the app yet he had given up on after a couple of months because of recieveing no matches at all. On closer inspection of his old Tinder profile it was clear to me why his first attempt had fallen so flat!

Martin had started his profile with no prior knowledge of how the app worked. He had set up and begun operating with just one poorly lit photo with no other details. His conclusion when he shut down his profile was simply that he wasn't good looking enough and girls were just not interested in him. It was a tragic way to end his first try at Tinder, and had knocked his confidence not just for interacting with girls but in everyday life. Improper use of Tinder has probably led to countless stories similar to Martins one so if his story seems familiar, never fear, there are plenty of ways to remedy your lack of success. Martin had embarked on the app without much consideration of quality of photo or presence of written details but with just a few minor adjustments and four days back on Tinder with a new profile, he got his first match!

For his main profile picture we chose one of him playing cards outside a coffee shop, taken whilst travelling through Europe in holiday. It was chosen as the picture was well framed and gave a good true representation of his looks, as well as the travelling element alluding to life experience, adventure and ambition;

incredibly attractive qualities to the opposite sex. Picture two was a wide shot of him on top of a mountain during a day out with friends hiking, beautiful scenery and him in the center with a backpack on. Again, this was reinforcing a sense of adventure. The third was of him DJing at a club night which he did in his spare time.

A big oversight with his original profile was his reluctance to show his profession. The reason was simply that he didn't feel it would be any relevance on an app such as this, but the reality is quite the opposite. As a lawyer, he held a job in a highly regarded profession that, unknown to him, could work very well in forming a complete image of himself and his lifestyle. After a bit of hesitation, I convinced him to disclose it.

For the bio we played around with a number of ideas and settled on simply a jokey pun based on cards, in reference to him pictured playing cards in his main profile. Being more of an understated kind of guy, he liked the idea of keeping the written bio simple and humorous.

So going from a profile with a poor picture and no information, we were now working with:

- A clear and well composed lead picture
- Interesting pictures showing particular interests
- Employment information showed he had a highly skilled career
- Education showed he had attended a prestigious university
- A short but humorous bio kept his description light and easy to read

So a two month drought of no matches can easily yield some success with just a couple of well thought out tweaks.

Thick Skin. Deal With It.

The world of Tinder requires somewhat of a thick skin. Without taking these following factors into consideration you could quickly find yourself becoming a bit disheartened with certain aspects so please read!

I barely get any matches even though I swipe right a lot!

The simple fact of the matter is that girls are much more selective on Tinder than guys and statistically swipe right a *lot* less. So don't see it as a personal problem, it's math. Tinder allows its users to be as picky and selective as they like. With the knowledge of the sheer volume of choice out there, users are undoubtedly driven to being extremely choosy and dismissive of the tiniest uncertainties about each person they see pass by on the screen.

Sometimes I'm talking to a match and they suddenly just stop chatting and I never hear from her again.

This happens all too often for most people. The only real downside to Tinder is the fact it makes one-to-one chats, with the ease and volume at which some girls have at gaining matches, a commodity that can be dismissed all too quickly. Sometimes if you don't hold a girls attention they can lose patience very fast. They are aware they can get a new conversation going very quickly. It's part of the game, do not take it too seriously!

Height. The inescapable stat!

Height for guys has become quite the contentious issue on Tinder. We've all seen some girls status' reading '*If you're under 6 foot don't even bother*' and other such damning statements pop up from time to time. It could be easy to become disheartened by such viewpoints, especially if we're conscious of a lack of height, as it's one thing that we can't change about ourselves even if we wanted to. The main thing to keep in mind is, not all girls think like that. Just the same as us guys aren't *all* one dimensional and prejudiced if a girl doesn't look like a supermodel.

Height in general can be a bit of a hang up for some guys but in terms of Tinder, it's not an aspect of your life that needs to be disclosed on your profile. By putting it up you're pandering to girls who are especially concerned with it and also displaying that you yourself are qualifying their prejudice and accepting that it's an attribute that you are willing to be or should be judged upon. In terms of your photos, they should neither disguise your height with clever angles, nor should *you* overly state your true height if you happen to be over 6 foot.
At the end of the day you want to be judged on aspects of your personality and it's inescapable not to be judged on your looks as is the nature of Tinder but don't feel pressure with factors such as height.

How To Deal With Being The Short Guy

If you are a 5'3" guy and disclose it on your bio, you will probably put off a lot of girls even if they don't have a particularly acute preference or prejudice towards height. If you feel it necessary for girls to know that you're a bit lacking in the height department, there are much more subtle ways to put this across without displaying it as weakness in your overall desirability. The best course of action is to reveal it gently. The last photo in your photo list is a good place to put a group photo with you and friends as it shows your sociable side and this could also be used to show your height in relative to your peers. If she feels strongly enough about your height being an issue then she might choose to pass on you at this stage. However if she likes what she sees in the preceding photos and your bio then she is less likely to make such a snappy superficial decision.

If height is an issue or a deal breaker for a match that you get, the subject will more than likely come up through the course of your conversation. If so, there's no point lying about it, as it will only make a subsequent meet up all the more awkward if you have falsified your height. It's good to be mindful that there are always going to be drawbacks to putting yourself out into the dating world, and with Tinder you will at times almost certainly encounter rejections based on fairly superficial elements. The key to success within this world is to not let those incidents affect your self-confidence. After all, one girls particular opinion on a certain aspect of someones appearance or lifestyle doesn't speak for every girl in the world, so never allow yourself to be fooled into thinking it is.

Failure and How To Easily Overcome It

Not every Tinder user has success. Guys will get the app, throw up a profile, swipe like mad with no good matches and quickly write it off as a failure.

Some won't get a single match for some time and feel incredibly dejected. It can easily become yet another episode in the erosion of their self-confidence. They might feel ugly and worthless, having had no success in finding the correct scenario or setting to interact with girls and now the online selection has rejected them too. It could compound their belief that they will be doomed to the single life forever.

Lack of success in Tinder is almost *never* just down to looks. Of course on the surface it is a superficial app that operates primarily on the assessment of looks and more attractive people are going to have more success, but using the tactics covered in this book (and bringing in a little patience) there is absolutely no reason you cannot find what you are looking for.

Work The System

If you look at the reputation of Tinder from a slightly different angle, the app that appears so superficial on the surface actually contains subtleties that give the user opportunity to promote themselves effectively beyond just a photo.

- Profession
- Education
- Bio (infinite descriptive possibilities)

The reason why these elements are so effective is down to the landscape of the app itself. Unlike other dating sites and apps that require vast swathes of information in order to activate your profile, Tinder limits the information its users can disclose. This limitation benefits users as it gives much great value to the pieces of information, which are able to be quickly absorbed by the potential match.

It's A Match – Now The Real Work Begins!

How To Win At The Initial Chat

The dream scenario is thus. A surge of excitement hits you as you see that *'It's a Match!'* screen appearing. She is attractive, her photos and bio suggest she's a fun girl with a good sense of humor and shares some of your interests. Your profile has obviously caught her eye and she's willing to get to know you a little bit more, so here comes *the* crucial moment of your Tinder experience with a girl; the first chat!

In front of you is an exciting prospect, but the thing to be aware of is at this stage it is still just a *prospect*. The connection hasn't been forged at the match; it is merely an opportunity to pursue a victory flag. This stage it actually even more important that your profile setup. Your first words to her are going to be a defining mark in her assessment of you. Remember, the pace at which Tinder sets people up is as fast as it is easy to ignore and move on from a match, therefore your first contact with her needs to stand out from other potential matches in a similar way that your profile did for her. So what are the best ways to initiate conversation? Here in the 21st century, we are the closest we've ever been here in the western world to equality amongst the sexes, but in terms of the old tradition of guys making the first move, it's still overwhelmingly the main thing in the world of Tinder. Remember how many guys are on Tinder as opposed to girls. Women have the upper hand with the numbers game. This is fact.

Rapport does not form immediately; it relies on consistently engaging conversation with time in between to allow positive opinions to form. Jumping straight in and saying *'hey you're really hot, do you want to meet for a drink tonight?'* is certainly bold and daring but not allowing any time for the girl to develop any sort of sense of your character will lead to dead ends. Instead, pace your conversation.

The Worst Opening Line Ever. It Always Fails!

Don't use the *'Hi how are you?'*. It is a common mistake to initiate conversation in this way. Although you might think the first text to a match is fairly unimportant, aside from her existing image of you, it will be a strong indicator to how confident you are and a line like that is uninspiring and just plain dull. Remember with any match that you might have, she could have countless other guys in her current chat feed, so to prevent yourself being lost somewhere down that long list of past matches, it's crucial to stand out from the crowd. Don't forget, you've already technically said hello by swiping right so there is no harm in skipping pleasantries and just asking questions about her or commenting on an aspect of her profile whilst connecting any common interests. For instance, if you both happen to be into snowboarding and you've noticed it from one of her pictures, you could open straight away with *'Nice board', 'Where is the snowboarding picture from? I was in Whistler a couple of months back it was incredible.'*

The Winning Factor...Humor!

Open with something a little outrageous but funny at the same time. You could simply say something about a stupid thing that happened to you one day. The opening line I used once was *'I've been sweating my ass off all day at work, how's your day been so far?'*. With something like this you are asking a question but framing it with something a little light-hearted but also a little intriguing as to what you do. It's all about catching your matches attention at this stage. A funny line to initiate can help break the ice. By both swiping right you have both declared interest in one another so a little humor to begin can help to alleviate any nerves about the first chat. Your first exchanges will set the tone for the course of the chat, and why not keep it fun and playful? Girls are much more at ease meeting a new guy if the conversation begins light hearted whereas a conversation opening with sexual references or anything overtly suggestive is only going to put her off, 99% of the time.

Find Out About Her

Just like interacting with a girl face to face, it's incredibly important to show interest in her. By showing interest right from the get go you'll stand a much better chance of getting the opportunity to develop a rapport. So with your match, ask questions about herself, career, short term and long term plans, places she's travelled to, music she likes. Exchanging these sorts of details will help to establish how much you have in common and the flow of the conversation will be a good indicator of the how good the rapport is between you. The questions like the ones I cited above are good starting points, however study her profile a little as this can help you determine topics of particular questions. After all, if she has spent time crafting that image of herself on her profile that she wants guys to notice, she will appreciate you picking up on the nuances. She might have quite different interests or job to you but don't be shy about asking questions.

Although things in common are a bonus in terms of initial conversation, interacting with someone from a very different walk of life can be exciting and enticing. Tinder has that wonderful quality of throwing all different types of people into the mix. You will encounter girls of all ages (based on your preference) colors, creeds and backgrounds and it's a great way to discover the variety out there, just as it is for the girls.

How To Move Things Forward Quickly

With the workings of Tinder in mind and the knowledge that any girl you are chatting to could have a string of guys in conversation at any one time, it's important to move the conversation on swiftly to avoid it stagnating. Once you have established a good rapport, don't be afraid to be direct and ask to meet up. It shows that you're interested in the conversation being more than just a fun chat on the app and will put her opinion of you to the test more than a hundred questions ever could.

'I'm free this Thursday and will be around town if you fancied meeting up for a drink?'. Or a less immediate approach could be

'I'm super busy with work for the next few days but I'd love to meet up if you were free sometime next week?'

Be prepared to face the fact they uou're not always going to get the desired response. She might be on Tinder purely to chat and interact with guys with absolutely no desire to be meeting up with any of her matches. It's better to find this out sooner rather than allow a conversation to drag out for a week only for it to go cold.

Dealing With Rejection

Getting a match doesn't automatically ensure riveting conversation or even her responding at all. There are a whole host of reasons why a match might not ever reply so I wouldn't dwell on it too much. I know of many female users who didn't respond to matches and often received angry and a little aggressive texts as a result, so don't be that guy! (aka A DICK).

At the end of the day Tinder can be just a game for some people and they might not treat connections seriously or even take someone's feelings into consideration. It's important to be aware of this so you don't get disheartened by the experience. A thick skin and a sense of humor can go a long way in the world of Tinder. We'll explore the nature of rejection on Tinder in the next chapter and the various ways you can accept and adapt to the less positive side of chatting with matches.

Be Direct But Don't Be A Creep!

Being direct and forward can be exciting and effective if your match is on the same wavelength, but if you are being overtly sexual or suggestive and it isn't reciprocated it will be a massive turn off for her. There are plenty of people on Tinder who use is expressly for hook ups and if you are one of them it is a delicate art in judging whether the match you are talking to is in the same realm. Also, be aware that though you might think you are talking one-to-one with a girl after matching, there's a chance she's sitting with a group of her friends and they are all participating in the chat and you are a dating guinea pig. So if you are going down the direct approach of talking about sex straight away and giving intimate details only go there if you can accurately judge she's on the same page and that you're not Tuesday evening entertainment for a group of giggling girls over a few bottles of white wine.

Let's Talk About Sex!

Talking directly about sex is a risky move, even if you feel she matches your desire to arrange a hookup. The reason being that talking about sex over text before your first face-to-face meeting puts unnecessary pressure on her about the expectation of intimacy, no matter how much she would like it to happen. The best time to introduce thoughts about sex or intimacy should be saved for that face-to-face meeting when you are able to more accurately gauge how serious your match is about pursuing intimacy early on.

Getting it right and being able to chat and maintain good conversation on Tinder is a bit of an art form and you're not necessarily going to work an A game in your first chat, it can take a while to build up the confidence and experience. We will encounter a good example of this in the next chapter, seeing how a guy, faced with a potentially fiery and attractive match, used his ability to remain restrained during their initial conversations to progress his initial connection into an unforgettable hookup with a girl. The sort of woman he usually would have deemed completely out of his league! He achieved this by simply portraying himself genuine and calm, while the majority of her Tinder world consisted of overly sexual and suggestive guys that made her crave some normal conversation and interaction.

Will & The Model

Will could barely believe his eyes. Staring back at him from a mysterious obscure picture was a girl of near absolute perfection. His heart leapt, eyes ever widening at each picture he scrolled through. He had never encountered a girl anywhere the magnitude of her in all six months since he had signed up to Tinder. So as he swiped his finger right, he sent a little prayer to the dating gods, any gods that might give him this opportunity. He nearly dropped his phone as the match screen flashed up in front of him. It was genuine disbelief followed by a wave of excitement, fear and anticipation.

Will, a decent looking guy in his late 20's, had started on Tinder after various relationship droughts and misadventures from the past two years. He had dated a couple of girls on and off but he was finding it hard to dedicate sufficient time that it required to maintain the relationships as a result of his dedication to the art that he poured himself into producing. A little starved of female contact and casual intimacy, he looked to Tinder to see what sort of success it could yield.

In matching with Laura, he had uncovered potentially the greatest test of his dating skills that he had been gathering throughout his adult life. The task was daunting but having had six months of chatting to various girls, without knowing he had been amassing new skills on Tinder that would soon have him embarking on the wildest week of his dating life.

Will had chosen his profile pictures well. Growing up by the ocean, he was a keen artist, a musician in a band, enjoyed the outdoors and he managed to portray all these aspects of himself through the pictures. His bio reflected his passion in all things art. He wasn't especially wealthy, nor had a prestigious powerful job but it was the sincerity in his words and pictures that initially attracted Laura, who identified similarly as a creative, artsy person. Little did Will know, but she was also an extremely well known model from overseas who happened to be travelling and visiting near his city at the time.

Laura had been travelling for a couple of months because of her job, bouncing between photoshoots and appearances, so any interactions with people were strictly business, and any social ones were the unwanted advances of horny guys who didn't conduct themselves with any decorum whatsoever. The same went for her Tinder matches. She would practically match every single one of her right swipes so it was a given that she had her pick of men on and off the app. Despite the uniquely fun aspects of her career, the travel was exhausting as was the lack of meaningful interaction with guys. She was lonely. Out of the hoards of attractive matches she had gathered over her travels, Wills profile intrigued her somewhat. There was no bravado or any overly boastful elements to his personality. He seemed down to earth and as she swiped she hoped the same over-sexed nonsense from countless previous matches wasn't going to play out from this connection.

The chat was initiated by Will, who established common interests quickly. The conversation flowed well over the next 48 hours. In that time he made no remarks about her good looks or pryed too much into her private life, instead focusing on her passions and interests while gradually revealing aspects of himself that he felt would interest her. Music and art were constantly recurring subjects and they quickly developed a rapport around the shared passions. Being an extremely attractive girl who was used to constant advances, it was refreshing to talk to a guy about shared interests and not just figuring out inventive ways to accept a barrage of compliments. Will knew the ball was in her court and knew that anything suggestive or pushy would turn her right off. He felt the only tactic in the success of this match was patience. And it paid off.

By the evening of the second day, Will took the initiative by saying *'So when are you going to come visit me?'*

Will couldn't believe what he was reading, and rather than jump right in, chose to make a joke about being busy, ending with an indirect compliment by saying how if she was half as attractive in real life it would still be definitely worth the trip. Rather than break with his laid back approach prior to her suggestion of meeting, he maintained the distance, bringing the compliment in gently without seeming like an excited schoolboy. Laura enjoyed the fact there was a chase. He wasn't presenting like the countless guys offering themselves up on a plate did. Perhaps he would need winning over?

This shift from her usual experience with guys was the crucial element to Wills success with succeeding in seducing Laura. A girl so attractive never had to put any effort in to make guys want her, and suddenly she was faced with just that.

Lessons Learned

* Don't need an illustrious career to hook a really hot girl.
* Keep cool (don't come across like a randy schoolboy)
* Enjoy the chaos and fleeting opportunity that Tinder can present to you.
* Stand your ground and keep yourself on level pegging, remain chivalrous but avoid coming across overly meek.

How To Progress The Chat Beyond Tinder

Tinder is incredibly powerful, and as we've seen so far, allows you access and to be accessed by countless girls from all walks of life in your immediate vicinity. So the conversation is going well, you have a bit of a rapport going and you're back and forth messaging throughout the day. It's somewhere here that lies the next crucial stage of using Tinder, which is in fact to get off Tinder. Every Tinder conversation will have it's own flow and progress at it's own pace, however what you must consider is that for every hour that you are speaking to your match on Tinder, she could be having a multitude of simultaneous conversations with her other matches.

Offer Your Number

Once you have built up a sufficient rapport with your match you can move the conversation forward by saying something like *'You seem really cool, here's my number if you want to catch me on there?'*. Offering her your number creates an important shift in the relationship in that it removes some of the pressure from her in the uncertainty of moving forward. It is similar to you making the first move with initiating conversation.

Call Her

The benefit of this move is the simple fact that in recent years, actual phone calls have been swept aside by the mountain of social media platforms, and increasingly, people conduct much more communications in this way. There is a bit of a lost romance in the phone call, and it will probably come as quite a nice surprise for her to get a phone call from you rather than just a continuous stream of texts. Calling her will also make you come across as more decisive and interested, and in the course of a phone call you'll much more likely to get a sense if she's genuinely interested in meeting for a date.

The Emotional Side

A hugely important aspect to why men and women interact differently in general, lies in how the sexes employ emotions in how

they interact. Understanding the differences in this use of emotions is critical in potential success with your matches.
A big disconnect for women when interacting with men is the frustration that men don't interact with the same level of emotion as they do. If we are talking in general terms, womens decision making, whether it be choices on relationships, material items, career options or whatever else will be influenced with much more emotional consideration. Hence the much publicized differences between men and women, often characterized through humorous scenarios; A woman worries her partner is quiet and conjures countless different reasons and potentially catastrophic motives behind it, yet all he's thinking about is what he wants to have for dinner or whether he left his car unlocked.

Although this is a fairly coarse generalization there is a lot of truth in that statement and many men and women would probably agree in accepting this division as a fairly broad yet accurate reality.
So how do you apply this to your approach to Tinder? By merely acknowledging the differences and applying that knowledge in your conversations you should be able to interact with each match a little more fluidly.

Take for example a conversation you might have about something you both enjoy, like keeping fit. Your typical response to question from your match such as '*Do you play much sport?*' will mainly go like *'I've always played a lot of sport since school, basketball mostly in school but I'm really more into trail running these days.'*

Factual and informative, which is how most guys operate. You're not quite fully engaging a girl who tends to respond better to answers, which incorporate an emotional response. So the same answer could be delivered in this way; *'Yeah I loved basketball when I was at school, nowadays I'm much more into trail running, it's great for getting rid of stress and shaking off a week in the office.'*
With this response you have delivered the same factual information yet formed it with your emotional motivation for your activities, which a girl will relate much more to.

Don't Be A Douche

The internet is a vast source of knowledge for pretty much anything your mind can conjure up and the same goes for opinion on how to use Tinder. There are unfortunately all too many jacked up, macho and frankly chauvinistic approaches out there to absorb if you're not careful. Tinder is a platform for quickly connecting with the opposite sex, and whatever ambitions you have within Tinder whether it's no string attached sex or searching for a relationship, the one unwavering factor should be your respect for those you are in contact with.

You don't score any points for being rude or offensive to the girls you are talking to, there are no moral victories to hurling abuse at a girl who has suddenly gone quiet on your chat and isn't responding. The only outcome of that will be her telling all her friends that she was chatting to a guy on Tinder who turned out to be a psycho and for them to avoid you like the plague! By the same token, if a girl decides to get at you about something, there is always the block function on the chat. Discard any girls who are acting stupid. The block function, although cold and direct, allows you to move on from unwarranted conversations, But just be kind if you have given up on a girl for whatever reason! Be polite before hitting that button. It doesn't take much.

Don't Get Too Deep

You want to save some of the more deeper elements of your discussion and divulging of information for your first meeting in real life. Don't blow it all during the phone chat as it's vital you can have a fluid conversation face-to-face. If you already know everything about one another you might find yourselves twiddling thumbs and losing the vital traction that is required in the early stages of a relationship, one-night-stand or more.

The Perfect Chat

Chatting to a match will feel intimate enough but she could be easily comparing you to other guys as you speak. So it is important to move your conversation away from Tinder as soon as it feels right and statistically the best success with matches comes from moving off Tinder within the first 48 hours or less. Once you're out of the Tinder chat window, any time spent on further dialogue between you is time away from Tinder itself and you put yourself in a much better position for her to view you separately from her other matches.

She's going to keep using Tinder even if the conversation moves to whatsapp or text messages. She's likely going to keep using it even after you've met up face-to-face. Tinder is the perfect tool for keeping ones options open, it's the escape plan for any new but floundering porrly matched relationship. But the sooner you can move the conversation off Tinder and into a neutral medium, the better chance you stand of her maintaining interest in you.

Meeting face-to-face quickly separates you from the rest of the matches. Also taking the initiative and instigating a face-to-face meet up shows you are keen, mature and driven enough to take it further. The most important thing is that it shows you are interested in her. Otherwise you're just another face in a long line of matches, insignificant and soon to be forgotten.
Remember, amazing girls are out there! You just need them to pay attention long enough to get to know you without losing interest.

Timing. The Vital Key!

Timing is a very useful consideration to apply in general when using Tinder after matching and you should be constantly mindful of the following moments. Here are a number of crucial points during your chats with your matches that will impact heavily on whether each chat will be a win or a lose.

How soon should I begin chatting after we match, or should I wait till she texts?

As I have mentioned a couple of times throughout the course of the book, a safe bet is to always take the lead with progressing the chat, right from the get go. So messaging her first will almost always be a good thing. Unless you're physically incapacitated and unable to get to your phone, it's better to start the conversation fairly soon after the match. Within the first hour or two at the most is as far as you should leave it. And also be mindful that, along with your match, she probably has a number of matches currently active on her account, so the old dating technique of leaving it 48 hours before you call to keep them keen doesn't really apply in the world of Tinder.

Are there any bad times to text?

Unless you work night-club hours or night shifts and are just replying to her last text, texting in the middle of the night will come across as a little creepy. Texting late during a night out in that sort of hopeful Dutch courage *'maybe she's out as well and would be up for hooking up'* way will only work if she is looking for the same sort of thing. It's a VERY risky tactic.

Whoops I made a bad joke or said something awkward, what do I do?

Tinder text conversations are delicate things. The block button is but a touch away and unfortunately she's going to use it if she gets even a whiff of doubt about you. Tinder is a filtering system designed to be continually cycling through new people, keeping the good ones and discarding the bad ones. It's going to feel like the equivalent of a girl turning her back and ignoring your advances in the middle of a bar. So the key to salvaging stuff is, in the event of saying something a bit cringe, don’t wait for her to respond in the hope that she sees the funny side and is willing to see past your awkwardness. Get straight in, diffuse the comment and move on. She might go cold or block you anyway but at least attempt to correct your text transgressions, don’t leave it up to her mercy!

The Risk Taker and How He Made It Work

Confidence is a huge feather in the bow of any guy when it comes to interacting with girls. Some guys can walk up to any girl on the street and strike up a conversation with fairly consistent success. It's a fearless trait that scares the majority of guys who could never fathom such risky moves. The fact of the matter is most men and women have issues with self-confidence in some area of their social interactions and it manifests itself most commonly when it comes to pursuing the opposite sex. The fear of having our advances openly rejected by someone we find attractive can be truly terrifying, causing people to clam up and be more passive. The benefit of Tinder is that it provides a barrier in which to act with more confidence than perhaps you would have in everyday life situations. There are no awkward mannerisms, nervous gesturing or stuttered speech to seal your ill-fate and thus you can craft your interaction with a girl from the safety of the chat window, asking questions you might normally be too shy to put across.

In Johns case, a good looking guy in his early 30's, who although worked in an interesting and outgoing role in the music industry, often found himself unable to initiate conversation with girls normally. He managed to find unprecedented success on Tinder by simply capitalizing on that attribute of Tinder which allowed the user to hide their pre-existing hang ups with interaction with girls. After becoming single following a fairly serious relationship, he took to Tinder in order to interact with girls again and look for girls to hook up with.

In his profile he mixed a well taken and clear lead photo with some humorous photos, along with a one line bio referencing a picture of his piece of crap car in one of the photos. This balance of a clear representation of himself and a bit of humor helped him gather a significant amount of matches, and from here, through trial and error, crafted an interesting and direct approach to propositioning his matches, leading to regular dates and hookups. He had a clear plan with his Tinder usage in that he had no desire for anything further than intimate relations and made no references to relationships or anything further. The clear and uncomplicated manner in which he presented and conducted himself, along with a genuine yet humorous profile were the keys to his successes in enjoying the benefits of what the app could bring, and he enjoyed them with like-minded matches who knew where they stood.

Q: With the girls that you ended up hooking up with just for sex, how quickly were you able to identify they were on the same page as you and was it your initiation of the proposition of sex or theirs?

J: Other than once it was always mine and always over text first. My shyness in real life would have destroyed that unless I'm sure the girl is up for it, which then makes me ultra confident - the defense shield of the app made it possible for me to ask.
I will say though that I think I'm pretty good at reading people and only once did I make a very bold move over text and was totally wrong about it.
As for how quickly, usually within a few hours but sometimes almost immediately. I did tend to go for girls my age though and stay away from younger. By my age or close to my age girls are more confident and sorted and will say what they want easier. They know what they want.

Q: Has your success on Tinder and the way in which it allowed you to conduct yourself and be more forward with girls made you more confident in general or is the confidence you were able to put across confined to the workings of the app itself?

J: It is the success with girls in REAL LIFE, brought on by the initial spark of meeting on Tinder which has made me more confident. Just matching with girls has not effected by confidence either way but Tinder gave me the spark I needed to actually meet the girls. So it was my own ability to date a girl who gave me the confidence, not the app, but I would not have got that far without the app in the first place.

Q: How much time/emphasis if any at all did you place on your profile pictures and bio? Did they provide useful points for conversations to start?

J: I don't think I spent loads of time other than just trying hard not to come across like a dick! I avoided really obvious *"I am cool, look, I tour with a band"* pictures but definitely put up images which hinted that I did something different. Through Tinder and in real life I have always played a slightly self-depreciating role, (sprinkled with moments of massive ego!) which girls liked, it was different from the usual guys…the trick is not to go too far down that road or you look weak.

John's formula for success was not pre-existing. It was trial and error that helped narrow his searches and matches into finding his optimum place on the Tinder scale.

Success on Tinder is based a lot on how much effort you put in; if you create a limited profile with no information, you'll get the bare minimum of matches, and if you're not too bothered on how you come across once you do get chatting, you'll see conversations run dry pretty quickly. Whereas if you compose a well thought out profile and really invest time into your conversations, soon you'll start to interact better with girls on Tinder and in Johns case, you'll benefit from it in the real world.

Meeting In Person – Making It Happen and Doing It Right!

Setting a date - again, YOU should take the initiative on this one. There are a number of things that can make you come across as flaky and leaving things open about a date in the hope that she will set it up or even have the desire to do so, comes across as indecisive. This is especially true if you initiated the conversation in the first place. It's only right really that you are the one to suggest the idea of a date. Every first date is a gamble; no amount of texting or calls beforehand can completely ensure you will hit it off on the night.

Some guys will like to focus their attention on just one match at a time, especially if they have a good feeling that the girl might lead to more than just a hook up. However if you are chatting with a multitude of matches at a time, and lining up several dates throughout the course of a week, your bank balance is going to be pretty light very quickly if you're taking expensive options.

So working on the premise that chivalry isn't totally dead these days and you were thinking of offering to pay for some or all of the check, then dinner at the Ritz and drinks in the hottest bar in town might not be the most economical option if you suddenly find yourself faced with a girl that you have not hit it off with and regret matching with. Keeping it casual and inexpensive will also lessen any pressure the girl will be feeling towards what she perceives is your expectation of how the night will go. A girl wants to feel safe and comfortable when meeting a guy for the first time and any hints of obligations perceived by an expensive first date will interfere with establishing a good rapport.

Meeting up in person is really the last frontier of the Tinder experience. By this stage you're into face-to-face interaction, the true test of your compatibility and mutual attraction. So the only thing for your Tinder profile to do now is to match up convincingly with the you in reality. As I stressed earlier in the book, sincerity is a key factor in the dating game as a whole. Deception is rife and commonly stems from a general lack of self-confidence or the fear that the person on the other end will be put off by an aspect of them. People resort to misinformation about their job and lifestyles, heavily editing or using tactically angled pictures of themselves to project the ideal image, rather than a true representation. Social media in general has predicated this idealistic portrayal of life. With any luck, you will meet matches that are as sincere as you are and you'll be able to enjoy the buzz of the good old fashioned face-to-face dating. After all that's the ultimate outcome of Tinder, making connections between people!

Tinder: Don't Be A Dick, Learn How To Use It Right and Win!

My mission with this book was to attempt to inform and inspire both brand new and existing users who were looking for ideas to breathe life into their profiles, with a view to gaining more success with Tinder. Throughout this book we have been slowly gathering a multitude of ideas and techniques for creating a succinct and attractive profile page, as well as methods in which to communicate with our matches after the initial connection. The real secret to this success is accepting the parameters that the apps mechanisms work within, and maximizing each and every aspect of that in order to come across the best that you can. The reality is that within Tinder you are assessed mainly on image and a short description but that it is an initial means to connecting with people and you would normally make your first impression on a girl by looks anyway.

Accepting that Tinder, despite some negative press on the grounds that it works very superficially, is in fact a powerful tool in meeting women and can lead to hook ups or relationships *when utilized properly*.

Remaining sincere with all your personal details and images to portray a realistic side of yourself is much more useful than trying to deceive potential matches just to increase your chances of initial matches or landing dates! Finding out you have provided false information will only have you frozen out of conversations or lead to awkward and humiliating face-to-face meet ups when they find out you're not quite the person you said you were.

With these factors in mind, it is good to be prepared to encounter girls that are employing those deceptive tactics, and learning not to lose heart after getting your hopes up with certain individuals. There are plenty of genuine girls amongst the false ones. Remember they are facing very similar problems and fears when embarking on Tinder themselves.

Accept that girls will be on Tinder for many different reasons and be using the app in vastly different ways, and that not every girl you interact with will be looking for exactly what you are. Not every interaction you have with a match on Tinder is going to end in a fiery sexual experience or wedding bells, just as not every girl you happen to meet in a bar will end those ways either.

No matter how much information you try to put into your profile in order for a potential match to correctly assess you, the reality is that it is impossible for her to really know whether or not the pair of you would be compatible. Even if every aspect of your profile ticks her boxes of the ideal man, she still has yet to see you face-to-face, hear you speak, study your mannerisms or have bodily contact. Those are the real tangible interactions that allow people to get a proper impression of who they are talking to and whether they feel a connection with that person.

With this in mind, we are aware that the profile that we put up, the combination of photographs and biography is merely a calling card. It is solely to entice potential matches. However the more honest you can make your profile the more likely you will match with girls who are on your wavelength or will generally pay any attention or time to you.

Tinder can't figure out whom your best match is…it just provides the venue for you to meet and you figure the rest out.

Presenting yourself through a mixture of humor and sincerity from your profile, and maintaining it throughout chats right through meeting up in person is the real key to success with Tinder. It's the key for dating in general. Consistency in your character will be hugely beneficial and give you the best shot at meeting and establishing relationships. Girls don't want to fall for a superhero and meet a chump in real life! Misleading a girl in the beginning will only disappoint further down the line. Being a millionaire space cowboy might get you more swipes initially but just as many rejections further down the road when they discover that you're not really whom you say you are. Whether you want to have casual sex or forge a relationship with your matches, you're much more likely to get there if on your first meeting face-to-face her initial impressions of you are *'he's just like I imagined he would be'* rather than, *'hmmm something doesn't quite add up, he definitely lied about things on his profile.'*

So go forth and swipe! I hope that you will be able to use the ideas from this book in improving your success not only on Tinder and getting matches, but that it also helps with the wider aspects of your social life in general. Self-confidence is such an indispensable strength in peoples lives but unfortunately there are just sometimes in our lives that we lack a little of it. So I hope that with any added success you may have with Tinder, whether it be through more matches because of your improved profile, to better conversations that lead to meet ups face to face will benefit your self-confidence as a whole and lead to a more fun, enjoyable and fulfilling life.

Chris Hemswith

Printed in Poland
by Amazon Fulfillment
Poland Sp. z o.o., Wrocław